Toxic
Flora

for Christine

Toxic Flora

Poems

Best wishes,

Kimiko Hahn

KIMIKO

HAHN

W. W. NORTON & COMPANY

New York   London

For information about permission to reproduce selections from this book,
write to Permissions, W. W. Norton & Company, Inc.,
500 Fifth Avenue, New York, NY 10110

For information about special discounts for bulk purchases, please contact
W. W. Norton Special Sales at specialsales@wwnorton.com or 800-233-4830

Manufacturing by Courier Wesford
Book design by Joanne Metsch
Production manager: Julia Druskin

Library of Congress Cataloging-in-Publication Data

Hahn, Kimiko, 1955–
Toxic fllora : poems / Kimiko Hahn.—1st ed.
    p. cm.
ISBN 978-0-393-07662-2
I. Title.
PS3558.A32357T69 2010
    811'.54—dc22

                                                2009052202

W. W. Norton & Company, Inc.
500 Fifth Avenue, New York, N.Y. 10110
www.wwnorton.com

W. W. Norton & Company Ltd.
Castle House, 75/76 Wells Street, London W1T 3QT

1 2 3 4 5 6 7 8 9 0

for Reiko

sticks feathers string mud

We trace analogies; as if it were
A joy to blend all contrarieties,

                    And to discover
In things the most unlike some qualities
Having relationship and family ties.

—from *Memoirs of the Life of Sir Humphry Davy*

Contents

•

•

•

Toxic
Flora

Nowadays when friends read about Darwin and something like *sexual cannibalism*, they immediately expect a poem. Then there's my own jealousy of the material itself: that someone will get to it first. Whatever the pressure, that the female mantis "devours the head of the still-mating male and then moves on to the rest of his body" is a shocking bit of information. Because I am past childbearing years? Because I have daughters? Or because it just seems vulgar to eat in bed?

On Deceit as Survival

Darwin could not believe an insect

would visit a blossom that had no reward
and insisted that the green-winged orchid

must withhold its nectar deep inside.
But he was deceived as well

since this orchid does not offer nectar

in its own Darwinian desire
to attract then rid itself of the useful bee.

Still others smell like feces or carrion

for the sort that prefers
to lay eggs in such environs.

Yet another species resembles

a female bumblebee,
ending in frustrated trysts—

or appears to be two fractious males
which also attracts—no surprise—

a third curious enough to join the fray.
What to make of highly evolved Beauty

bent on deception as survival—
liposuction, rejuvenated clitoris,

plumped lips? I plead with daughters

to forget the enhanced buttocks
and rely on soap as fragrance.

But, how can a mother instruct on deceit

when girls so readily flaunt thigh and thong?

and when parking lots are replete
with broken fences and the preternatural buzz of the car alarm?

Toxic Flora

There is something vital
about the *Passiflora aliriculata*,

which over a million years varied its cynogens

to discourage feasting insects

although the *Heliconius* butterfly
resolutely adapted to those same poisons

finally transmuting itself into one—

actually repelling predators
as it leisurely fluttered

from leaf to blossom
seeking out a spot for eggs.

What does this demonstrate about toxins
or residence?

Or carrying around a portion of the childhood home

where the father instructs the daughter on the uses of poison
then accuses her of being so potent?

Passion

The raflesia,
whose blossoms measure a yard across

and evolved from the poinsettia and passion family,
smells as rank as rotten flesh

so that carrion flies

searching for a stinking carcass
will assist in its pollination.

How to measure such passion
and which is the daughter as she phones from ferry or dormitory:

blossom or swarm?

Nepenthe

Quaff, oh quaff this kind nepenthe, . . .
—EDGAR ALLAN POE

The *Nepenthes rafflesiana*, or pitcher plant,
a bowl-shaped leaf with liquid at bottom,

acts like an animal predator to attract then digest insects
such as the itinerant ant that scouts around *the dry lip*

then bids colony members follow only to slip inside
owing to increased humidity or nectar secretion.

Scientists measure this completely passive phenomenon

using tiny electrical probes.
Just what is the reward for such studies?

botanical insights? lessons on symbiosis or unpredictability?

For me, more than the thought of wet lips
or Homer who mentioned Nepenthe

as a potion to dispel one's misery,

I think of memorizing poetry in the fourth grade:
Edgar Allan Poe, while longing to forget the lost Lenore,

composed verse after verse that implanted recollection.
That drug, that conductivity,

that pleasurable sensation of stumbling into memory.

Sibling Rivalry

When I suggest that everything is about sibling rivalry
he mocks me as if I were his sister. But

it's a little true, especially for the common wasp

Copidosoma floridanum.

Though it's bizarre that the mother lays her eggs
inside the egg of the cabbage looper moth

the real story is about the warring wasp larvae

split into two camps: the bloodsuckers
that drink the caterpillar's blood

and the sibling soldiers
that attack said bloodsuckers

which then remain cloistered to wither
inside the withering host. Furthermore,

it is the female soldier that more often eats a brother—

not rivalry so much as outright cannibalism.
Not unlike that friend's older sibling

———

obliterating everyone over dinner conversation. Still,

I know that not *everything* is about sibling rivalry
since the poor caterpillar's doom cannot be denied

and I told him so.

For the Affection of Ants

The way to elicit care
is scent

for the Alcon blue butterfly:
their progeny smells so identical

to those of two ant species
that the ants themselves

take the butterfly larvae to their nest,
where they feed them, and neglect their own.

As J.W. puts it, those butterflies are tricky motherfuckers!
And it's true although it's also true

one ant species is developing
a resistance to the larval infection,

by altering its own scent.
At times I'm wary of resistance

unless I catch myself
mistaking infection for my own offspring.

Cross Species

for M

My daughters' mix of *Mayflower* and plantation shit

that some do not appreciate,

elsewhere (car service, escalator, etc.)
is well eyeballed—

though the gen pop does not

get color.

In fact, color is not something *to get*:
suburban usage of

the *ah-so*, the *niga*,

the *how ghetto*.

I've always approached such white collar lexicon
with a silent *fuck off*

though I admit my own *Pleasantville*—

though when such a one actually demanded,
what about the children—?

I knew the comment really concerned The Colony Club,
say,

and not my children's bodies, lavish
from nymph to mutant wing.

Just Walk Away Renée

for M

The mite harvestman, a daddy longlegs

found in 400-million-year-old fossils,

has wandered between several continents
without so much as a swim. A conundrum

if it weren't for plate tectonics,

a notion only realized in 1911
when a scientist matched up fossils

on either side of the Atlantic.
I think about this discovery and try to tease out a simile

but really it's better just to leave
the first land animals alone. The shifting

and colliding and breaking apart alone.

The drifting. The sadness—
that marks the opening of a quest

only to discover estrangement.

Bumblebees

The foraging bee that doesn't make it
back to the hive

and companion warmth
fastens to a leaf.

Bumbling-bees?

Or does the nectar so distract

it forgets the cells
called home?

The lapse is a cause for concern
the entomologist reports—

because its tiny body slows to the stillness of dew.
Is that quiescence?

or acquiescence?

Or simple stupidity
one always forgets a day later?

The Apiculturalist

for C

In black veiled hat and canvas gauntlets
Jean Paucton, seventy, climbs the baroque stairs

of the Palais Garnier opera house,
to his rooftop apiary.

The theatrical prop man studied beekeeping
at the Jardin's venerable institute

then hauled onto the seventh-floor ledge
his five weathered crates—

swollen with honey, nearly a thousand pounds a year.

"The bees make an impression, do they not?"
he declares.

     And you, dear poet?

Your little apiary of simile and syntax—the busy bite
that separates truth from Truth?

Do you not weary of the student manuscript,
that makes elegance

but does nothing to sting cousin or twin? You

who do not flinch in or outside your own sweet studies?
The husband's soft skin? The vial of antidote?
It's a sadistic occupation, is it not?

Yellow Jackets—

protect through venom and candor.

While timing their own dinners
to mother's tray, father's tongs,

or baby's saucer-sized cheeks,

they can sting any intruder repeatedly
unlike the honeybee's suicidal sortie.

I like that. I like X
who calls people out at brunch

through simple narration:
your mouth never stops moving.

Or, *you eat off other plates as if they're your own.*

Or, *you check your BlackBerry when no one is talking about you.*
Or, *you laugh whenever you insult someone.*

A startling attribute I wish I could emulate
if only my sting possessed such integrity.

The Diaspora of Sadness

Reconsidering his collection of the Costa Rican butterfly

a biologist realized the *Astraptes fulgerator*
was in fact a complex of ten species

that occupies overlapping territories

because, although *a splash*
of iridescent blue scales across body and wings

appeared in all adults,
the caterpillars *looked quite different*

and preferred different plants
as if each had diverged

from distant ancestral species.

Which points to what?
That *none could stray from such advantage?*

That survival is as complex as, say,
the melanin and melancholia

of my mother, a field hand's daughter?

Amor

The armadillo eats ants

and possesses a tough exterior.
In matters of such armor, Moore was expert

and, as suggested by Molesworth,
not as fortress

but as a means to set forth,
where Dickinson could not;

where it's okay to be covered with plates—

though perhaps, like Dickinson,

some just don't make it farther
than garden or paper;

where, what is armor
is lexicon—

the stranger, the more secure:

pangolin for one,
Quartz for the other.

For me: linoleum.
For Rei: spatula.

Miya can't decide
but believes it begins with an *m*.

On Butterflies

Only the rare butterfly eats
live things:

the *Hyposmocoma*'s caterpillar
weaves silk around a mollusk

fastening the shell to a leaf
then sticks its head inside,

eating the snail alive.

An entomologist on Maui
likens this freakish behavior

to a wolf that dives for clams.

I see it as a little girl
who tears apart a little friend

to eat his entrails.
Or a mother who rips open another mother

for her unborn child.
Or a mother who rips open her own infant

to release the demon inside.
This hunger is less rare

than a butterfly with sharp teeth.
My mother is from Maui.

Sustenance

The Madagascan moth alights on the sleeping Magpie
insinuating its proboscis between the closed eyelids

and sipping out tears for nearly an hour.

Unlike other moths who use a soft-tipped snout,
those of the *Hemiceratoides hieroglyphica*

are like harpoons with tiny spines and barbs

causing scientists to speculate about nourishment
and ignore what begs greater pursuit—

why a sleeping creature might cooperate
in its own melodrama and ache.

Perhaps it's just bad karma
since these birds refused Noah's ark

and did not weep at Christ's crucifixion.
A darling friend profoundly understands

since she makes her livelihood exacting pain.

Ipomoea Purpurea

The farmers revile the glorious flower
whose noxious vine reduces crop yield.
The resolute blossoms prosper

beyond the scientists' active flavors
meant to rid the world of such discord—
the farmers so revile these glorious flowers.

I don't envy the researchers' herbicidal pressure,
though it's kept them in labs for a decade.
The resolute blossoms prosper

while the pertinent vegetables of farm labor
prove stunningly fragile in the fragile field.
The farmers revile the glorious flowers—

for others, the wild *Ipomoea purpurea*,
is not the strangler weed.
Although fundamental blossoms do prosper.

Who mourns the dying or the dead—
the fate of the proletarian seed?
I, too, curse the glorious flower,
fundamental vines that rise and prosper.

In any case, the other day I thought, how
rapacious—which, by one definition means
unscrupulous, and by another, *live by eating
prey*.

Raptor

for M

Whether carried off to heaven or abducted then raped
the word conveys transport

and for the Great Gray Owl,
renouncing the belt of spruce in the far north

to follow the red-backed vole.
It's an irription of historic proportion

so much so that the low-flying hunters
are colliding with vehicles—

a different transport than *rapt* or *rapture*

unless one is a scientist or birder
or etymologist

capturing import as it migrates
with rodents.

Literally with rodents, but suffering
a tendency toward the rapacious

which I think was M's concern
when he asked at an Asian bistro

my thoughts on the proximity of climax to heaven.

Defining *Syrinx*

Migrate with an ornithologist
and life will come to *sod farms and mudholes*

where shorebirds scavenge in soggy pits for worms and insects
before transequatorial flight—

a shadowy sojourn using *magnetic field, starlight, and other*
  biocompasses.

Their migratory calls, differing from routine song,
are *high pitched and clipped,*

each burst, a fraction of a second.

Dr. Irby Lovette finds a link between such vocalization
and the particular syrinx behind it.

And what *is* a syrinx? A bird's vocal organ,

a pathological tube in the human brain,

a narrow corridor in ancient Egyptian tombs,
a reedy shepherd pipe,

and, if capitalized,
the figure who, in order to protect her chastity from Pan,

was transformed into the reed from which he created the panpipe.

Unlike the capacity for migration which can be lost and
    regained,
the mountain nymph was forever rooted

in this pitiable swamp. Please recall
I warned you earlier

that muck is where a lover's sojourn leads to.

Swinburne Island

We collect what we collect with varying intent
from mammy dolls to gall wasps;
and for a fledgling ornithologist, cormorant vomit,

or what his advisor describes as
frantic ichthyology—a search for ear bones or other fragments
that could identify a certain species among the partially digested.

The handsome Devil Birds that dive like penguins
and fly like ducks are drying their spread wings
when Colin climbs onto some rocks

just below the Verrazano-Narrows. On Swinburne Island
once a quarantine for immigrants, now rubble,
the young man sees the birds flushed from thickets

and hears the dumping of stomach contents—
which they do to lighten for takeoff or signal, *Get lost.*
Or flaunt what's been consumed:

Grandma Ida's wienerschnitzel. Uncle Jack's Sunday comics.
Auntie Kimiye's pearls. Burying a tiny terrier up to its neck
but just for ten minutes. A little sister's blanket.

A thump, smelling of mummified fish remains
and prized by an ambitious graduate student
whose own gut is frantic with fortune, *tangy and rotten.*

Allure

Unlike most birds, the Loggerhead Shrike,
or *Butcher Bird*,

isn't thwarted by the horned lizard
whose sharp skull spurs can pierce a throat.

Rather, the male impales those reptiles

on thorns or barbed wire—
displaying a larder for the ladies!

I know about such demonstrations:
the volumes on lust murder

my beloved bestowed on me that first brunch—
indicating a backlist.

That was it.

I had a few collections myself:
one flaunted fishnets, another

a penchant for antique dental instruments.

You know what I'm talking about.

Awareness

Among the burrowing owl's
scraps of carpet and tinfoil

tucked into the humid straw,
the hoard of cow dung is especially prized

as it attracts dung beetles.

The owls watch for hours
revealing a tool of attraction

of which those clever creatures

may not be aware.
What then *is* awareness?

Connecting shit to consequence:
the flicker that links, say,

chlorine to climax—
or who consumed whom at faculty picnics.

On Fidelity

Australian magpie-larks that couple and clasp
produce an *alternating antiphonal song*

that coalesces into the call of one—
an indication of how long the pair have sung duets

and how faithfully they'll synchronize a defense of turf—
which makes sense, though so unsure of my own part

I'm as ready to take off in torment
as I am to beat off any competitor

for a nest of twigs, trinkets, and assurances.
But you've heard this lament before.

The Perpetuation of Sorrow

When we *fragment forests*
we create an excellent habitat for the cowbird

whose females shove the eggs out from songbird nests

and substitute their own
for those full-time mothers to hatch.

A spiral for which I am sorry.
I couldn't help myself.

I'd forgotten that I had saved the article until I began clearing out several years' worth of clippings. It was mid-August and H had just noticed two praying mantises fastened together, front to back, on a sedum stalk. I looked, too, but didn't linger—although I did return the next day to check for evidence on the ground.

The Fever

for L

The coral reefs are changing color,
the black and crimson bleached away:
the ocean's rising fever,

in every drop the seas over,
damages the membrane of symbiotic algae
and coral reefs change their color.

True, it's less sensational than acts of terror.
True, we can slather sunblock then sunbathe
despite the ocean's rising fever.

After all, the planet isn't boiling over;
algae is not an inflamed country.
It's just coral reefs, changing color.

I wonder if it's, yet again, the ozone layer
ruined by my aunt's persistent use of hairspray—
this ocean's rising fever.

I already own my share of vivid jewelry
from Mother's childhood village on Maui.
Still, the living are losing color
in my ocean's escalating fever.

Demeter's Cuttings

My own mother taught me suspicion:
to question a man's gifts, whether trifles or truffles.

She also taught me the names of trees
and how to rub off

the dried sheaths of silver dollar stalks—
toss the seeds back over the bed.

She didn't teach me much else, and truthfully
I like nature—not to tend but visit,

to watch it take care of itself.
Still, a fist full of snapdragons—

a flock of yellow dragonflies—

a cluster of cicada nymphs—

this is what I wish to entice my daughter back to:
what I love to what I love

while below, the subway quakes the whole building.

•

Once she called to tell me, *Mother, don't make me choose.*

A young man had taken her into the subway
to his parents' home for dinner

and by curfew she called to say there were no cabs in sight.

I said, *But you're too young to stay with him.*

And I imagined him standing over her
as she covered the receiver, saying—

My mother won't let me stay.

(Where was the father? Teaching his new wife's son to piss
    in a pot?)

•

What I've learned about men is that they bludgeon
to make a point: that he will not shut up

until his woman weeps and folds in on herself.
Blames herself for his empty hands. Then

he can dismiss her—or hold her,
as if rescuing her from himself. This

is what I learn, daily, to walk away from:

shut up, you're wrong. Who cares. And now

in my own apartment I wait past her curfew
to doze or leaf through *People*, *Self*, or *Us*;

listen to restaurant crowds dispersing,
the drunks heaving below my window;

wait up to hear a car door. I know

that first boy takes a turbulent daughter
to keep her in the dark

but still I wait for keys at the door.

Was she so bored in these rooms cluttered
with scarves and cosmetics? A few African violets?

And isn't that all right—to be a child and be bored?

•

My own childhood was a doll

that could do nothing but close her eyes,

games with nothing but dice and "men,"
a tape recorder to record—what? That boredom?

•

Then there were records of myths and *Peter Pan*.

The marsh across the street.
Cattails. Jack-in-the-pulpits.

And trees so high you couldn't climb them.

Or if you did, the jays would peck your head
to protect their squawky nests.

Then there was the odd heron.
Then there was her father.

•

Before she met this young man, I asked,
Do you miss me when we're apart?

and she answered, *I miss myself, Mommy.*
These days she claims, *I'll do what I want.*

•

In spite of the blue porcelain cups,
the kittykat clock hung on the wall, its tail ticking—

there comes a point
where the mother must risk losing her daughter

by telling her, *No, you must leave him tonight.*

My own sisters tell me, *She'll come home.*
And when she does, the morning glory vine

on the construction fencing across the street
will open its pink lyric.

Then we'll toast bread and perk coffee

and arrange the asphodel on the yellow table.

Or will she regard the welt on her arm
as an exotic flower from that other world—

I cannot say.

Was the coital cannibalism shocking because
I'd thought it only occurred in captivity?
Nevertheless—as my father-in-law used to say.

Maude

Although the exoplanet Gliese 436b
orbiting around Gliese 436

may possess a livable zone
in between its fixed-sunny and -frigid sides,

it still does not possess a more transcendent name.

I'm interested in whether this exoplanet possesses atmosphere
as much as the next person—

but more, I'd like my daughter
to watch for the wobbles

that a planet's gravity creates
in the motion of its stars

and name these masses after family members:

Kimiko would be a great name—
but really, I'm thinking *Maude*.

Planet Maude.

To imagine qualities would be to suggest
the obvious attributes

a daughter might bestow on her mother,

my mother. But rather than be obvious
I could take pleasure in naming any planet after her—

though, if pressed,
I imagine one as petite, habitable, remote,

and owning a number of moons.

An atmosphere surely.
There was a short time I wanted the same daughter

to go into mycology—
to name a fungus

after the men in the family.
I don't think either would be asking too much.

The Search for Names

The right to name Planet X belonged to the Lowell Observatory
where the Kansas farm boy engaged

to photograph night heavens using a blink comparator

quickly suggested *Slipher*, after his superior.
The widow, Constance Lowell, suggested *Zeus*, *Lowell*, and
    Constance.

Then eleven-year-old Venetia Burney
put forward *Pluto*, ruler of the underworld

(as well a dark and cold terrain)
and a god who could turn invisible.

She was eating breakfast with her grandfather, Falconer Maden,
when he read about the search in the dailies.

Lucky girl. Fortunate planet. Exultant netherworld.

Speaking of Orbiting—

Galileo first observed the rings as rings in 1610
but did not know what to make of them

suggesting that Saturn possessed *ears*.
Not until a more powerful instrument in 1655

did Huygen solve the mystery—
though a contemporary theologian

believed the rings to be Jesus's holy foreskin

ascended into the heavens.

Amazing how we use fluid and flesh
to quench our questions:

maybe the rings are fetuses,
maybe the rings are strands of my mother's hair,

maybe the rings are the uterine linings from my dried up uterus,
maybe the rings are saliva from apologies never uttered
    to my husbands for leaving without explanation,

maybe the rings are baby teeth, wisdom teeth, vomit, and shit.
Maybe the rings are you when you decide I'm not what you
    bargained for.

I favor the holy foreskin for some reason.

The Transit of Venus—

is not about love. It's about an eclipse
and measuring the size of the solar system

using Johannes Kepler's seventeenth-century formula.
And since the sightings offer

the chance to read Venus's atmosphere,
it's about *rarity and exit position.*

Fluctuation. Signature. Rivalry.

More than entertainment or retraction,
it's about reflection—

what we recall before real memory recedes.

Candy after potty chair? Threshold before shotgun?
Who got to walk out first and who got to last?

My Very Exciting Magic Carpet Just
Sailed Under Nine Palace Elephants

for J

Before the recent conference on Pluto's status
a planet appeared beyond number nine, not to be seen again.

Since then, Pluto's been demoted
from full-fledged to *dwarf planet*;

and a planet, heretofore undefined,

is *any object in orbit around the Sun*
that is dominant in its immediate neighborhood—

though from my viewpoint
if a body is not considered a planet

then it shouldn't be called *a dwarf planet*.
It should have its own category altogether.

(Maybe *rockette*
since scientists are so enamored of female names.)

Thankfully, we needn't wait for the definition of a dwarf
    planet—
something about *self-gravity*, *rigid body forces*, and *planetesimals*.

But what in the world is a *planetesimal*
and how to mourn the loss of my *Elegant Mother*?

Stardust

Although the pressure of starlight
blows dust out of the system,

the constant banging and colliding of planetoids
creates *new dust*

which winds out in a thin outer doughnut.

And from these *disks of gas*
a planet forms and the dust clears away.

Fascinating, all this debris
circulating in our own fringes,

giving rise to zodiacal light

and a reason for developing sharper telescopes:

the father spanking the ten-year-old
just out of the shower

and because she already had breast buds

she didn't want anyone to look.
Years later, the whole family still thinking it was funny,

I think—*so what!*

Scientists also suggest the dust clears out
from the tug of an unseen companion.

Space

for W

I don't understand space—the emptiness,

the distance measured in light.

Take the protostar: I can't grasp
how clouds of dust and gas can collapse

then suck up more stuff and expand

to over twenty times the size of our Sun.
In all this heat and shadow

where did Mother disappear
after the car crash? Where

is my daughters' grandmother
since they've learned there is no heaven—

except for rose, hedge, and pine?

What kind of astral influence is it
where in varying degrees of reversal

a thing breaks down
yet shows no sign of ceasing?

And what now is the nature of her form?

Refuse

Scientists now observe that Saturn's largest moon

boasts a substantial orange atmosphere
and is inscrutable to the human eye.

Will their spinning camera detect lakes
of liquid methane? Regions of ice water?

What we do know is that Saturn

(not the one with rings of ice and rock)

ate his children rather than die in supreme betrayal;

that it is difficult to see things
from the child's vantage

though one was a child previously.
This makes me sad.

And I wonder about surface features—
the dark and light craters

seen with unprecedented clarity.

The mostly pure ice.

The fields of clouds.
Or children turning into orbiting debris,

I think that fathers think.

The Fate of the Cosmos

Identifying a 1572 supernova blast as a new star,
Tycho Brahe shattered the Aristotelian opinion

that the heavens above the Moon are immutable.

Now these explosions are signal markers
in the fate of the cosmos:

that a mysterious "dark energy" is wrenching space apart

which means that how the stars explode
has more to do with a daughter's need to speak her mind—

what can be wrenching—and for whom.
And, does it finally matter?

Sedna

Come to find out, Sedna
is the Inuit woman

whose father cast her from their kayak,
thus transforming her into the spirit of the sea—

but also the name of 2003 VB12,

a planet or something beyond Pluto.
It is the first body to be discovered

in the Oort Cloud, *a hypothetical region
of icy objects that become comets.*

But questions remain: how
can a region be hypothetical?

how can a scientist not know

what a planet is? how could a father
throw his daughter from a kayak

even if she did write poetry
that hurt his feelings?

I am not sorry.
He always said, *art comes first.*

But that is a murky region

for fathers and daughters—
what comes first.

And what my daughters wish to know is
did she drown for his sake

or to learn how depths betray?

Perhaps my fascination with sexual cannibalism has to do with ritual—to which animals, like ourselves, must submit. The definition on my laptop dictionary: "A set sequence of actions that an animal uses to communicate information or to reinforce social cohesion." But is a rite or ceremony necessarily cohesive? And for whom? Just what is the serial killer, male or female, communicating? Is it too clichéd to note that such bloodlust coincides with religious gesture?

Heteralocha Acutirostris

When the stunning huia became scarce,
Maori priests would declare a ban
on killing these small black birds, so prized
their tail feathers were presented as mementos
and worn in battle and funeral rites.
But the Europeans ignored the priests
and soon the Maori themselves did not listen.
So now, the males with their short sharp beaks
to drill through bark and the females
with their long bowed ones to pluck out the grubs
have perished but for museum specimens.
Is this how we admire success in pairing—
kill then stuff then display as exemplar?
Ah, my beloved, hold fast to me, in terror.

Xenicus Longipes

The four known species of bush wren in New Zealand
are, by now, endangered or extinct.
Possessing trifling tails and wings, none fly far—
instead they hop and dart
in whatever undergrowth scrapes the landscape.
Those on Cook Strait's margin of rock
entirely lost the capacity for flight
and in 1894 were destroyed not by farmers,
hunters, pet traders, rats, disease,
natural disaster or want of food—
but by Tibbles, the lighthouse keeper's cat.
Oh, what we think we need to survive kills others:
I have consuming need for my beloved, he knows—
and I hope he is not sorry.

Aepyornis Maximus

Remarkable that the elephant bird—
encountered and documented by Étienne de Flacourt
the French governor of Madagascar in 1648—
at ten feet and one thousand pounds
was smaller than a New Zealand moa!
A bird for crying out loud!
Extraordinary that its egg,
largest on record, measured a foot long—
the monstrous mother and newborn possibly inspiring
those in the Arabian tale of Sinbad. But most
breathtaking is that the bird is no longer with us
except in museum exhibits and archaeological sites—
the way my first marriage feels like someone else's colony
in someone else's fervent geography.

Cyanopsitta Spixii

Every skin that remained of the Spix's Macaw
evinced a death in captivity
and a history usurped by farmers and trappers
among the trees of inland Brazil.
How extreme to be so prized
that price kept one's species thin
until a single male remained in those forests.
Recent attempts to foster regeneration
by introducing a once-captive female
were never successful: the survivor
was last seen saving his fascination
for a macaw of another species. In the wild
that can happen to the point of extinction—
I know myself.

Conuropsis Carolinensis

A small green parakeet named Incas,
the last of its kind, died in the Cincinnati Zoo
a week after Valentine's Day, 1918,
barely surviving Lady Jane, his mate
of thirty-two years. The only parrots to adapt
to unkind North American winters, hundreds
would consume entire fruit farms.
The birds were shot to protect such crops
as well for sport and for their sultry feathers
suitable for ladies' hats. Hovering and squawking—
rather than abandon the dead—they made an easy target:
how hunters care less, and oh,
how one falls extinct for love!
I recall my mother's untold affection.

Pinguinus Impennis

Large, flightless, and defenseless,
the great auk was captured
for feathers for featherbeds—
hunters loosening the plumage in cauldrons
fueled with the oil
from the freshly killed auks before them.
After the 1830 volcanic eruption in Iceland, after
museums and collectors vied for the near
extinct "penguin of the North,"
in 1844, the last pair was beaten to their deaths
and their solitary egg dashed on the rocks of Eldey Island.
Could we not sleep on straw or goose down?
What dreams are worth such extinction?
And are they dreams I'd wish to own?

Does the female eat the male to insure the most poignant father is spent on their own offspring? Or merely out of hunger as in the case of non-courtship cannibalism? Stephen Jay Gould suggested they might simply mistake the male for prey. But, personally, I don't think a female would mistake a male depositing sperm inside her as prey. A necessary nuisance, perhaps. Or a competitor for food. Or even a convenient snack. Gould also felt the submission theory was an example of biologists being "overzealous about the power and range of selection by trying to attribute every significant form and behavior to its direct action."

On Being Coy

Many fish in the murky ocean caves
of Mexico, Brazil, Croatia, and Oman

have no eyes
though in the streams outside—

clear as a frat bar in '75—

other males zip around and nip the females

to test chemical signals
and harass

with so much sex

that the females often cease to exist.
Better off

with a slower, blind suitor

I say—then think of Marvell's *rough strife*—
which I adore.

See—a little coyness *can* work
to cloud the current.

Those black lizard boots instead of mules—
that Manhattan tourist spot.

He's twenty-five. I'm forty.
He demands one thing—well, two: my feet.

See what I mean?
Little has changed in the carpe diem
or the simmering transparent stream.

660 Degrees Fahrenheit

How not to adore extremes—

in scalding volcanic fissures
fathoms below our surface—

those extremophiles, thriving and delighted?

Where else the ardent vent?

The ardent?
The venting?

Ode to 52 Hz

While monitoring enemy subs in the Pacific,
hydrophones classified a distinct

basso profundo frequency
calling with a metronome's regularity

as belonging to a whale, species unknown.

For twelve years he's been calling out to no response.
And now Mary Ann Daher,

the pioneer in marine mammal acoustics

who spent years eavesdropping
on the largely hidden lives of whales,

has died. So who will listen to 52 hertz?

To what scientists suggest
is either a hybrid great blue and fin or malformed?

Or as my husband (who has only studied Melville)
suggests, is a mutant? Me—

I responded to a Japanese American
but we divorced because

it doesn't always work out according to kind
though I miss saying to my first mother-in-law: *tadaima*—

a frequency I cannot return to.

Of course I'm being a Romantic—
thinking the whale cared.

That *it knew*. That it cried out to a human
since no others listened.

That it knew no others listened—
or feared as much.

That we think so and can bear sentimentality.
That we listen for such opportunities. With frequency.

Admission

Victor Hugo claimed that *the dream*
is the aquarium of the night

confirming for the tourist
the mysterious hush

when viewing the depths sealed behind plate glass.
Even more than dream, I wish

to name the various species;
to stare or flee the one that sports a playmate's face

blinking back at me. Cathedral of science!
Cathedral of childhood! Of childhood nights!

Of adult—what? Of remorse as a hall
to which we pay admission?

Brooding

for N

Misinformation lasts millennia. As when a student
hauling a trawl bucket from the black mid-waters off Monterey

found a mass of squid eggs with the mother beside them—

surely a coincidence
since female squids abandon their eggs.

Then a year later, another bucket produced the same—
this time hatchlings—though general disbelief continued.

So the scientist lowered a robot with camera and lights
and spied a female cradling several thousand eggs,

waving her tentacles to aerate and nourish.

Misconceptions about squid arise
because the deep is so poorly explored;

that one might substitute one's own fear
for hard evidence. My own daughters declare

if you'd been around more we would've gone mad—

which is somehow comforting. Cuttlefish
are next under scrutiny.

From "The Evolution of Feeding"

Most ray-finned fish use suction and a set of bones
—*pharyngeal jaws*—to eat.

According to experts on fish biomechanics,
the moray eel

—a ray-finned fish without fins—
does one better:

after the front jaw snaps down,
it releases the prey to a second set

that shoots forward then recoils into the throat

dragging the meat with it.

Voila! this deity from the depths
combines vagina dentata and phallus

into the exquisite realization of male and female *as one.*

Here the water is salty and frigid
and so dark you can't see its red.

The Blob

In 1896—nearly fifty years after Melville's masterpiece,
three years before Freud's *Dream*
and my grandpa's journey across the Pacific—
a storm shoved seven tons of white blob
onto a St. Augustine shore:
twenty-three monstrous feet of glistening flesh—
a surviving archaist or alien
or devil of the deep.
Chunks were immediately shipped to the nascent Smithsonian
for display then storage;
until, one hundred years later, a Florida scientist
examined the same specimen, as well as
new blobs floated up from the depths—
declaring the cryptozoological curios merely
the remains of large cetaceans.
The narrative of the stupefying has closed with
nothing more than pure collagen
washed up from the ocean's unconscious. *Sad to say.*

Phrases: *an evolutionary advantage to being eaten,*
passing on their genes if they cooperate in their
own death, surrendering themselves to their mates,
encourage their own cannibalism, go along with
their own demise, benefits of sacrificing themselves,
complicit in their own deaths.

The Sweetwater Caverns

Curious to see caverns,
we detoured in Tennessee
to ramble through Fat Man's Misery,
past a ballroom and gun powder machine
till we reached The World's Second Largest Underground
    Lake—
on which my husband had promised a ride
in a glass-bottom boat.

There, a kid hunched over a hot-rod magazine.
Dan, I think his name was,
radiant in clammy, artificial light.

I asked Dan, *college break?*
He nodded inside his hoodie
then helped me into the glass-bottom hold.
I peered into the milky water
and watched the seeded trout swim up for the chum
he dumped overboard on our account.

He was milky white himself,
from months of cave sitting.

I wondered if he'd write a poem
on a summer spent underground.
Thought to suggest it—how foolish—
then wondered if what I really wanted was Dan,

as I stepped into his boat, to take my arm and ask me
    something—

at this middle age, probably for a couple coins
then give a promise of safe passage
as he ferried me to the realm of the dead

that I've been thinking about for several years
not because of a girlfriend's cancer
but because my body is no longer young.
I mean, lovely—
and that there's no turning back to that water's edge.
There's only the couch
every afternoon at four o'clock
and not wanting to ever move. Not wishing to die exactly—
just not wanting to rise
because the light feels so pressured. And I can't have
that ardent glow reflected back while brushing teeth
or fastening a necklace. Now there's this

casting around for other stuff—
the daughters' secrets—the pathetic urge to write about their
    secrets—

or a crush on Charon. Not an old man as it turns out
but a youth, colorless and tired of his iPod.

No, he's not really of interest to me.
And this is my secret: that I wish he were—
as with those arms

reaching through clouds of cigarette smoke
to lead me into reeking dives.

I'm past that. And he, Dan,
not the poetic Charon—
will probably climb out of the caverns
into the six o'clock evening sun. Stretch. Change his shirt,
eat his mother's meatloaf and head off in a rusted Honda
for the Piggly Wiggly parking lot
with a six-pack and a girl,

those hand-sized moths flitting in the light
as the sheriff chases the kids to another dead-end spot—

those enormous dusty moths my husband caught
for me to hold in my hand
because he knows, in the afternoon light after the dank caverns,
how fluttery the furry wings will feel.
Which is more than melodrama can bear.

To have wished for Dan *to ask me something?*
I know *the passage* is not what you wanted to hear.

The Extinction of Frogs

It is hard to document extinction.

—DR. CHRISTOPHER J. RAXWORTHY

A trace might lead to interference
of, say, oxygen

then thirty-two strains of fungi—

evidence recollecting extinction after the fact:
off-putting soap, cake crumbs,

a case of something noir

and certainly, sudden disaffection arising

on South Dodge or South Davenport.

(Everything leads to infection.)

Hoping to inhibit the decline,
curators house the golden poison dart

and Argentine horned frogs for good measure.
Some disappeared

without so much as a birthday card—

hazard. It was South *Hazard*.

I'd told him I was sick of it all.

A second example: "Male Australian redback spiders
court females for up to eight hours by plucking the
strands of their web. Once a male starts to mate, he
promptly somersaults onto her fangs. He continues
to mate as she feeds on him. In some cases, the male
crawls a short distance away, courts the female again,
and then mates a second time. He flips onto her fangs,
and by the end of the second mating he is dead." *Som-
ersault* is a curious term here, unless viewing the ety-
mology from the Spanish, *sobresalto*, "a sudden assault,
a surprise."

A third example: Similarly, the orb-weaving spider
dies as it mates, leaving its sexual organ "stuck in
the female's receptacle." But is this really a strategy?
Doesn't strategy imply consciousness? As if every orb-
weaving male wishes to die and be eaten down to its
sexual organ?

Origin of the Head

Was it only 3 billion years ago
that the Earth, spinning without inhabitants,

first sprung a single-cell organism,
then issued multicelled algae, then

a wormlike organization of cells
until, millions of years later

insects and reptiles appeared?
Somewhere in this span

a sensory trap evolved

that efficiently met its prey—
later evolving the *I want to eat you*

to *I want you.*
Then to the popular, *I want you to want me.*

And now this love poem
so my man will cherish the brain

as well the thigh-highs, the thong, and head.

Or is desire still so rudimentary—

little more than an opening
with quicker and quicker reactions

for which I am, more or less, thankful.

Big Feathered Hats

worn by women a century ago
would necessitate aligning the body in a threshold

just so. It's this *just so*

that intrigues Professor Iriki,
who has probed clumps of tissue

to uncover how cells and circuits

map the world around it

to the body's schema.
To sense that tight spot

whether concrete
or like the night her lover admitted

he'd had an affair with his own mother—
his word, *affair*—

and she knew in her bones
which was really her brain

that she should get the fuck out.
Those feathers. That exit.

Pink

From experiments on thirteen dead pigs
buried six months in a bog

then exhumed to note levels of preservation
here's a lesson on limited exposure:

one was reduced to fragments, another exploded when touched.

I, too, preserve loss
whether catching the pink piglet at the county fair

or swinging the gondola atop the pink Ferris wheel
that decomposing summer

and, in its pink twilight, going off on a tear

with the town coroner who ruled against rapture two nights in a
    row
and couldn't abide slinky blouses.

Turning Points

Returning through channels, sailors guide their boat

by keeping red buoys on the right.
Pharoah ants, who follow pheromone trails,

utilize branch-angles at an ambiguous point.

But how did a key locate lock and sink?
how did a ball of wet clothes

find the shower stall?
and how did the body find its mattress—

the night that B and I celebrated respective divorces?
Avenue A was a treacherous strip:

which is to say, how does one discern

which fork in the road leads to sensational calm—
the other, to seasonal ruin?

I wonder still, who or what acted as a sign?

Phantosmia

The persistence might be turpentine for her,

Old Spice for you—this not relinquishing trauma,
accident or, say, benign humor.

Does she wish to walk away
from the room aerated with a pungency,

invisible and fatherly?
She tries to tell the nose to trust the nose:

It's gone, the can of paint brushes!
Still, she is not allowed to withdraw

from that disorder of newspaper and tarpaulin
as if mildew were a means to affix.

I can't

stop wondering if something was meant to smell sweet
or humiliate.

The Soul

I addicted myself to the opening of heads.
—THOMAS WILLIS

A physician of King Charles the Second,
Willis was intrigued by *the curious quilted ball,*

receiver of animal electricity—
but could not bring himself to identify the brain

as the bodily home of the soul.
But why cite region

on behalf of invisible impulse?
What prompts one child

to warn her mother
that she doesn't want to read about her affairs

with boys in muscle cars

but that she is glad to know
the collections will survive her

as a keepsake of extreme explanation—

and prompts the other
to write so viciously of family vacations

the father renounces her?

Why open the skull as daily enterprise?
Why research what is transparent?

Why not see the soul for what it is—
that sideswipe? that rip tide? that addiction

to human remains?

Cope's Rule

for Harold

According to Edward Drinker Cope,
nineteenth-century paleontologist, fossil records show

lineages become larger over millennia

indicating that bigger is more successful.
Though later scientists *offered further support for Cope's rule,*

from mammals to corals,

paleontologists in the last century challenged such evidence.
Gould, in particular, was dismissive

of such a *psychological artifact.*

Current more rigorous studies suggest
the results are plain to see:

being big provides a big advantage. And yet,
the study continues

Why isn't Cope's rule more of a rule?

Laws of physics reveal *that insects*
cannot grow to the size of Tyrannosaurus rex

because their exoskeleton cannot support
heavy loads of body mass. Furthermore, a small rat

is probably better adapted to a certain niche.
There is also the issue of surviving mass extinction

though not everything *can get small enough quick enough.*
I am small already so that isn't a personal concern;

still, each consecutive husband has gotten larger
though I'm not sure why or what that reveals

except it's easier for Harold to reach for stuff on the top shelf
rather than watch me, at fifty, climb on the kitchen counter,

though last weekend he bought, for us both, a step ladder

ruling out vulgar advantage.

Alba

December before sunrise, I hear the morning
before opening my eyes to worn-flannel light:

scores of geese from the neighboring lake
lift the day into wakefulness, my guess

bound for winter fields uncovered by a thaw
and still flecked with grain. I hear

not honking but a roar that pours over our house

and wonder, before completely conscious,
why they haven't left in their V's for the south.

Instead they commute from pond to field and back

illustrating that we eradicate

the world's most brilliant routes;
that we might never have answers

regarding the cues that send animals on their way
even navigating vast distances to places they've never been.

Likewise, a complex dilemma for the red knot
flying from Tierra del Fuego to the Arctic—

and swarms of elk, dragonflies, zebras and leatherback turtles
that cross invisible routes.

Like reliance itself. Opening one's eyes to other questions
from caucus to kitchen. From daughter to granddaughter.

Counting on such a cry
someday waking me from down an invisible corridor.

Icebreaker

Scientists, unnerved by stretches of melted ice
around the North Pole,

cannot discern whether the pace of change
is mostly greenhouse gas or natural influence

missed in earlier forecasts.

Shipping magnates and drillers of oil
are not *displeased* for the now-watery sea routes

and care less how polar bears scavenge
to eat and reproduce. Ice retreat?

Ice deficit? Thawing permafrost?
Artic Oscillation?

That we cannot care beyond filling a gas tank
or wondering if a summer patio will be under water

may be the ironic side effect
of evolutionary biology. Or just plain narcissism.

Or just plain laziness or laxness.

Or just plain greed.
Or just plain brainlessness.

Or just plain lack of imagination.
That Arctic sinkhole.

A Meditation on Magnetic Fields

for S

Reversal is overdue: the last change of polar fields
occurred when man was carving stone into weapons.

We know the Earth's fluid core
of molten iron

emerges in a lava flow
as infinite tiny compasses

drawing South as a new North;

we know the random flip
depresses honeybees, Zambian mole rats,

homing pigeons, salmon, whales, frogs, newts,
bacteria, and crops. We know *the collapsing field*

sends polar auroras flaring to the equator.

We know it confuses baby loggerhead turtles
on their 8,000-mile swim around the Atlantic

using magnetic clues to check bearings.

Can you do something to save love
before much in the heavens and Earth go askew?

I wouldn't know—
except where I mean to make sense of *rocky memories*,

to continue text-messaging through the static.

Notes

The following poems are matched to the texts that inspired them. I hope I have not offended or misquoted any of the authors in any manner. One of my challenges was to live up to their own gorgeous and urgent writings.

The paragraphs between each section (marked by an asterisk in the contents) are inspired by "This Can't Be Love," Carl Zimmer, the *New York Times* (*NYT*), 9/5/06

"On Deceit as Survival"
"Orchid Sends a Not-So-Subtle Message to Bees . . . ," Carol Kaesuk Yoon, *NYT*, 4/6/04

"Toxic Flora"
"In Death-Defying Act . . . ," Nicholas Wade, *NYT*, 8/1/00

"Passion"
"Giant Stinking Flower . . . ," Carol Kaesuk Yoon, *NYT*, 1/27/04

"Nepenthe"
"A Slippery Slope Is the Secret Weapon of Some Pitcher Plants," Henry Fountain, *NYT*, 1/1/08

"Sibling Rivalry"
"Lessons from an Insect's Life Cycle: Extreme Sibling Rivalry," Carl Zimmer, *NYT*, 8/14/07

"For the Affection of Ants"
"Lessons from an Insect's Life Cycle . . . ," Carl Zimmer, *NYT*, 8/14/07

"Just Walk Away Renée"
"A Daddy Longlegs Tells the Story of the Continents' Big Shifts," Carl Zimmer, *NYT*, 8/28/07

"Bumblebees"
"Morning Light," Diane Ackerman, *NYT*, 8/24/04

"The Apiculturalist"
"Who's Humming at Opera?" Craig S. Smith, *NYT*, 6/26/03

"Yellow Jackets—"
"Selfless, Helpful and Intelligent: The Wasp . . . ," Natalie Angier, *NYT*, 8/17/99

"The Diaspora of Sadness"
"DNA Bar Coding Uncovers Secrets . . . ," Nicholas Wade, *NYT*, 9/28/04

"On Butterflies"
"Caterpillars That Could Use Herb Butter," Henry Fountain, *NYT*, 8/2/05

"Sustenance"
"Moths and a Drink of Tears," Henry Fountain, *NYT*, 1/16/07

"*Ipomoea Purpurea*"
"Mornings Not-So-Glory?" Henry Fountain, *NYT*, 8/24/04

"*Raptor*"
"In a Vast Hungry Wave . . . ," E. Vernon Laux, *NYT*, 3/8/05

"Defining *Syrinx*"
"Songs and Sojourns of the Season," Natalie Angier, *NYT*, 9/18/07

"Swinburne Island"
"Like Ducks and Penguins, with Nervous Stomachs," Ellen Barry and James Estrin, *NYT*, 8/22/07

"Allure"
"A Lance, a Lunch or a Mate," Donald G. McNeil Jr., *NYT*, 4/27/04

"Awareness"
"Décor as Bait," Henry Fountain, *NYT*, 9/7/04

"On Fidelity"
"The Quality of the Duet," Henry Fountain, *NYT*, 6/5/07

"The Perpetuation of Sorrow"
"The Forest Primeval Isn't . . . ," William K. Stevens, *NYT*, 9/24/95

"The Fever"
"Too Warm for Coral's Algae," Henry Fountain, *NYT*, 6/13/06

"Maude"
"All of a Sudden, the Neighborhood Looks a Lot Friendlier," Dennis
Overbye, *NYT*, 9/21/04, and "The Fungi Hunt . . . ," Bruce Barcott,
NYT, 9/7/04

"The Transit of Venus—"
"Venus Returns for Its Shining Hour," Warren E. Leary, *NYT*, 5/18/04

"My Very Exciting Magic Carpet Just Sailed Under Nine Palace Elephants"
"A Dwarf Planet Gets a Name," Kenneth Chang, *NYT*, 9/14/06

"Stardust"
"Watching as Dusty Disks . . . ," Dennis Overby, *NYT*, 12/21/04

"Space"
"Scientists Spy a Hungry Star," Henry Fountain, *NYT*, 5/18/04

"Refuse"
"Through Saturn's Haze . . . ," John Noble Wilford, *NYT*, 7/13/04

"The Fate of the Cosmos"
"Life-or-Death Question: How Supernovas Happen," Dennis Overbye,
NYT, 11/9/04

"Sedna"
"Planet or Not . . . ," Kenneth Chang and Dennis Overbye, *NYT*, 7/30/05

Sonnets on extinct birds are based on work in Rosamond Purcells's *Swift as
a Shadow*, Mariner Books, 1999.

"On Being Coy"
"In a Realm of Blind Fish . . . ," Carol Kaesuk Yoon, *NYT*, 4/20/04

"Ode to 52 Hz"
"A Song of Solitude," Andrew C. Revkin, *NYT*, 12/26/04

"Brooding"
"Scientists' Discovery in the Deep Casts Some Squid Mothers in a Brighter Light," William J. Broad, *NYT*, 12/20/05

"From 'The Evolution of Feeding' "
"If the First Bite Doesn't Do It, the Second One Will," Carl Zimmer, *NYT*, 9/11/07

"The Blob"
"Ogre? Octopus? Blobologists Solve an Ancient Mystery," William J. Broad, *NYT*, 7/27/04

"The Extinction of Frogs"
"Increasingly in Decline . . . ," Jane E. Brody, *NYT*, 6/29/04

"Origin of the Head"
"With an Evolutionary Milestone . . . ," Yudhijit Bhattacharjee, *NYT*, 2/18/03

"Big Feathered Hats"
"When the Brain Says, 'Don't Get Too Close,' " Sandra Blakeslee, *NYT*, 7/13/04

"Pink"
"Piglets Buried in Bogs a Clue to Mystery," Anahad S. O'Connor, *NYT*, 8 /17/99

"Turning Points"
"Better than a Trail of Bread Crumbs," Henry Fountain, *NYT*, 12/21/04

"Phantosmia"
"Q & A: Persistent Smells," C. Claiborne Ray, *NYT*, 6/22/04

"The Soul"
"How Mind Became Matter," book review of *Soul Made Flesh* by Carl Zimmer, Adam Zeman, *NYT Book Review*, 4/4/04

"Cope's Rule"
" 'Bigger Is Better' View of Evolution Gains Credence," Carl Zimmer, *NYT*, 12/28/04

"Alba"
"Migration Interrupted: Nature's Rhythms at Risk," Carl Zimmer, *NYT*, 1/1/08

"A Meditation on Magnetic Fields"
"Will Compasses Point South?" William J. Broad, *NYT*, 7/13/04

Acknowledgments

With heartfelt thanks to those who have read and reread these poems: Eamon Grennan, Nicole Cooley, Laure-Anne Bosselaar—and my beloved husband, Harold Schechter. As in previous collections, Jill Bialosky conjured splendid magic, for which I am grateful. And Miyako, "Cross Species" is for you, of course.

With thanks to the editors who first published these poems:

"*Ipomoea Purpurea*," *America Loomed Before Us: Contemporary Poems from the Other U.S.A.* (Smokestack Books)

"Maude," *Bamboo Ridge*

"Ode to 52 Hz," *Bamboo Ridge*

"The Perpetuation of Sorrow," *Barrow Street*

"Turning Points," *Barrow Street*

"Admission," *BOMB*

"Big Feathered Hats," *BOMB*

"Swinburne Island," *BOMB*

"Alba," *Cerise Press* (online literary journal)

"Allure," *Cerise Press*

"Awareness," *Cerise Press*

"*My Very Exciting Magic Carpet Just Sailed Under Nine Palace Elephants*," *Cerise Press*

"*Just Walk Away Renée*," *Clementine* (online literary journal)

"A Meditation on Magnetic Fields," *Clementine*

"Cross Species," *Columbia* (Columbia University)

"Speaking of Orbiting—," *Columbia*

"On Butterflies" (originally "Acts of Violence"), *Crate*

"Bumblebees," *Earth*

"Origin of the Head," *Great River Review*

"Passion," *Great River Review*

"Refuse," *Great River Review*

"The Blob," *Gulf Coast*

"On Deceit as Survival," *Gulf Coast*

"For the Affection of Ants," *Hanging Loose Magazine*

"Sibling Rivalry," *Hanging Loose Magazine*

"Sustenance," *Hanging Loose Magazine*

"Yellow Jackets—," *Hanging Loose Magazine*

"The Search for Names," *Jubilat*

"The Apiculturalist," *KR online*

"*Raptor*," *KR online*

"Space," *KR online*

"The Transit of Venus—," *Lumina*

"The Fever," *The New Yorker*

"On Being Coy," *The Paris Review*

"Cope's Rule," *PEN*

"Nepenthe," *PEN*

"On Fidelity" (originally "The Magpie Lark"), *PEN*

"*Amor*," *The Saint Ann's Review*

"Phantosmia," *Storyscape* (online literary journal)

"Sedna," *Storyscape*

"The Soul," *Storyscape*

"Pink," *TriQuarterly Review*

"*Toxic Flora*," *TriQuarterly Review*

"The Extinction of Frogs," *Washington Square*

"From 'The Evolution of Feeding,'" *Washington Square*

"660 Degrees Fahrenheit," *Washington Square*

"*Aepyornis Maximus*," "*Conuropsis Carolinensis*," "*Cyanopsitta Spixii*,"
    "*Heteralocha Acutirostris*," "*Pinguinus Impennis*," "*Xenicus Longipes*," *Wet:*
    A Journal of Proper Bathing (University of Miami)

The photographer commented, "It kind of got
boring. Then she reached around, grabbed him
around the neck and bit his face off."